# INNER HEALING

# INNER HEALING

**Michael Scanlan**

**PAULIST PRESS**
NEW YORK ● PARAMUS, N.J. ● TORONTO

Ex Parte Ordinis:
Nihil Obstat:
Christian Oravec, T.O.R.
Daniel Sinisi, T.O.R.
*Censors Librorum*

Imprimi Potest:
Columba Devlin, T.O.R.
*Minister Provincial*

Cover Design: Morris Berman.
Drawings: Gloria Ortiz.

Library of Congress
Catalog Card Number: 74-81901

ISBN: 0-8091-1846-7

Published by Paulist Press
*Editorial Office:* 1865 Broadway, N.Y., N.Y. 10023
*Business Office:* 400 Sette Drive, Paramus, N.J. 07652

Printed and bound in the
United States of America

# Contents

# Introduction

"This is what we proclaim to you: what was from the beginning, what we have heard, what we have seen with our eyes, what we have looked upon and our hands have touched—we speak of the word of life." (1 John 1:1)

The words of St. John speak eloquently of what this work attempts. I write to proclaim a message of faith, hope and love—a message of good news. It is not a complete message; it is confined to what I and others with whom I share my life have heard, have seen with our eyes, have looked upon and have touched with our hands. We have heard men and women cry out in agony, and emotional turmoil and we have heard them later sing out in peace and freedom. We have seen men and women appear as dead, as bound with chains of despair and self-hatred and we have seen them later appear as alive, as lights of hope reflecting a love for themselves and others. We have touched those trembling with fear and coldness and have touched them when the vibrations of love and the fire of the Spirit were flowing through their lives. We write of these things in hope that they will be words of life for all who read these pages. We have also seen many seek healing and apparently not find it. We have had to encounter the reality of these experiences.

We pray that the Word made flesh will bless each reader with the peace of Jesus Christ: the great gift which the world cannot give. The pronoun "we" appears frequently through this work because it is the truest expression of those whose convictions and opinions are being expressed. To use "I" would falsify the truth for I have drawn deeply from the discernment and insights of Father David Tickerhoof, T.O.R., Father Francis Mac-Nutt, O.P., Sister Margie McGuire, C.C.W., and Sister Ann Thérèse Shields, R.S.M. They have been a part of this work at such depth that their contributions cannot be precisely identified. At the same time, I alone am responsible for the final formulation of the manuscript.

"We" is also preferable to a third person expression in order to limit the statements to what we have experienced and not create false impressions of a universal scope to the truth of many statements. We recognize the competence of qualified counsellors and psychiatric therapists in their professional areas. We do not want to undermine the good being accomplished in those professional services: we hope to support and add to it. We hope that they will accept the validity of healing through that work of God we call the ministry of inner healing.

We also use the first person plural to state directly what hasn't happened for we are still waiting for the completion of many healings. At times we proceeded in the wrong way, by-passing some necessary step such as calling the subject to repentance and forgiveness. At times progress was slow and painful, extending over years. Other times the healing was immediate and filled with joy. We share only what we have learned and no more to the praise of the Father in the Lord Jesus, our healer.

Finally, we dedicate this work to all who carry the marks of suffering and sin, and in that wounded state have responded to the Lord's call to bring healing to others.

# I
# The Ministry of
# Inner Healing

"Is there anyone sick among you? He should ask for the presbyters of the Church. They in turn are to pray over him, anointing him with oil in the name of the Lord. This prayer uttered in faith will reclaim the one who is ill, and the Lord will restore him to health. If he has committed any sins, forgiveness will be his. Hence, declare your sins to one another and pray for one another that you may find healing." (James 5:13-16)

We wrote of inner healing in *The Power In Penance* (Ave Maria Press, 1972). We wrote there that wounds and scars on the inner being of men are the roots occasioning most of the sins presented in the sacrament of penance. We referred to self-hatred, inability to trust, guilt, anxieties, fear of the future, and repressed resentments as areas that give rise to such sinful behavior as fighting, quarrelling, crimes of violence, lust, greed, cheating, stealing and lying, as well as such states as alcoholism, drug addiction and suicidal compulsion. Priests and penitents, Catholics and non-Catholics wrote affirming the insights and approaches to healing contained in the booklet. Priests usually asked for another book developing the confessional approaches. Penitents wrote of the new freedom and peace in their lives and asked for the names of priests and other counselors who would help them and their friends to grow to greater wholeness and holiness. Non-Catholics wrote that the approach was successful as a format for counselling. Many Catholics wrote that the booklet had moved them to return to confession after a lapse of years and that the experience of being healed in the sacrament had led them to become regular penitents. The one general note in the letters was: "give us a deeper understanding of inner healing."

In the past two years, we have rejoiced to learn much more about inner healing. We have seen a pattern develop; we have learned to distinguish surface wounds from deep scars; we have learned to discern which of various approaches to the inner healing prayer is right for the situation; we have learned that all healing is to be viewed within the context of healing the whole man, which means discerning the will of God for the total person and his relationship within the whole body of Jesus Christ. Finally, we have learned to reverence the right time—the Lord's time in which the power of the Lord's love will heal.

We have also learned how much confusion surrounds the term "inner healing." Many people speak of any spiritual growth as an inner healing. They may refer to a counselling session, hearing a sermon, or a new prayer level as an inner healing experience. If an experience occasions a new sense of peace, love or freedom they will announce: "I have received an inner healing." Their responses might well be true. Nevertheless, a greater precision in language will better serve truth and through precision foster growth of the ministry of inner healing as distinct from other ministries.

## HEALING

"Healing" is something distinct from growth or a qualitative improvement. Healing means that process by which what is wounded or sick becomes whole and healthy. Healing has meaning in direct relationship to a negative situation of a specific hurt. Therefore, we do not speak of a teenager who is growing in height, strength and knowledge as being healed and we should not speak of general areas of growth in holiness as spiritual healings.

We should also note that healing is a naturally induced process to health. This does not require any intervening event which is not explainable by the observable laws of nature. Healings in themselves are subject to explanation through natural processes. A spiritual healing is a healing by which spiritual stimuli accelerate the natural processes. As such its spiritual source is seldom demonstrable to non-believers. Skeptics can always offer some natural explanation that could, regardless of how unlikely, explain the new state of health. A miracle, on the other hand, involves a change which cannot be explained through the ordinary operation of nature. It is against or outside the laws of nature. Healings can also be miracles but they need not be. When a spiritual healing is not a miracle, those with the gift of faith understand God's action while those who do not have such a gift of faith allow for natural explanations.

In our ministry, we have seen healings which convinced us that the power of the Lord directly caused the healing. The following healings were witnessed by a number of mature people; they were tested and found convincing but they were not miracles because natural medical explanations could be given for all.[1]

"A fifty-year-old man, retired from a steel plant because of impaired hearing, came for prayer. He had been to doctors who assured him that his hearing was so permanently damaged that no treatment or hearing aid could help. We prayed with him in response to a strong desire to help him coupled with an expectancy that the Lord would manifest his response to the prayer. Both the man and the minister immediately knew a special sense of God's presence. The next day the man began to hear normally and was able to return to work. The doctors responded that sometimes the body heals itself in these ways."

"A man was dying of malaria in the Amazon territory of Brazil unable to walk or eat. His temperature was dangerously high. His pulse was beating approximately twice as fast as normal. We travelled up river for two hours. We anointed him and continued healing prayers. We administered two aspirins and carried him to the boat. By the time we arrived at the mission station, he was healthy and apparently only suffering with fatigue."

"A six-month-baby, Darlene, was born deaf and examined by many doctors who could not prescribe a remedy. The baby was anointed in the sacrament of the sick as part of a longer prayer for healing. Two weeks later the father noticed the baby responding to sounds. The doctors examined the baby and found perfect hearing. The baby's hearing is continuing at a better than normal level and no signs of the original problem are in evidence."

"Another baby, Maria, was retarded from birth. The doctors had concluded that at best the retardation could be controlled but gave no hope for recovery. Examinations were scheduled for six-month intervals. A few days after one such examination, we were gathered for prayer. The group praying concluded that the Lord wanted us to pray for a healing. The next morning we brought Maria into our midst, placed hands on her and proclaimed "In the name of Jesus be healed." A sense of peace and blessing seemed to fill the room. A few days later Maria's mother convinced the doctor to reexamine her. The doctor found a sudden and unexplainable improvement. Maria now is a normal child achieving average grades in her elementary school class."

In the case of both babies, the doctors concluded that the treatments which they prescribed and which had produced no favorable results for an extended period of time must have suddenly taken effect. There was a possible natural explanation because the natural organs, which were not operating properly before, now were functioning in a healthy manner. There was a healing but not of a miraculous sort; therefore, it strengthened the faith of those who viewed it in supernatural faith but did not have a spiritual effect on those who viewed it from only a natural point of view.

We have seen allergies of many sorts—asthma, poor eyesight, damaged backs, and various respiratory diseases —healed and remain healed over a period of years. We mention these healings because they were in our lives or the lives of those we know intimately. We have prayed for many other ailments and have not observed any physical change. We have noticed that whenever we pray under a genuine impulse of expectant faith, something does happen. There is a spiritual or physical change. Sometimes there is a significant growth in patience or understanding of a higher good coming from the suffering; sometimes there is physical healing in conjunction with medical treatment. And sometimes there is physical healing independent of any discernible medical treatment.

When we pray in faith and compassion but without any special impulse of expectant faith on the part of the minister or person seeking healing, at times there is a healing, at times the person is convinced to change elements of his life but very many times, we do not observe any change. There are also times when in praising God together healings are given without specific prayer.

The experiences of our lives conform to our understanding of the teaching on healing in the New Testament. We read of four general statements of the Lord healing all who come to him.[2] We also note approximately thirty-six separate relatings of specific healings.[3]

Professor Morton Kelsey of the University of Notre Dame has done extensive research on the place of healing in Christianity. The conclusions from his book, *Healing and Christianity*, form a powerful call to present-day Christians to respond to this power in their midst.

> To sum up, we have found in most religions, including Judaism, an appreciation of nonphysical or spiritual realities that influence man's life and contribute to healing. But only in the New Testament tradition have we found a consistent practice of healing based on a fully developed understanding of God's love and a divine will for men. On this basis Western culture was founded, with the same unique interest in healing generally expressed.

> In brief: physical healing is a living process, and as such it is an inner mystery in the end known only to the cells themselves which are involved and to the one who created them. Thus, it is a process about which

we must keep learning as much as we can, both physically and spiritually.

In particular, healing occurs when the conditions are right. There are physical conditions which only the physician is qualified to know and prepare. There are also emotional conditions which can be made ready by those trained in psychotherapy. And finally, healing requires conditions of a spiritual nature which can best be seen and helped along by those trained and practiced in the unique traditions of the vital Christian Church. Together they make a team of which God has need.[4]

This book concerns specifically the healing of the inner man. So at this point, we narrow our considerations to inner healing and then further to the ministering of this healing.

## INNER HEALING

Inner healing is the healing of the inner man. By inner man we mean the intellectual, volitional and affective areas commonly referred to as mind, will and heart but including such other areas as related to emotions, psyche, soul and spirit. Inner healing is distinguished from outer healing commonly called physical healing.

We believe that inner healing is clearly found within the ministry of Jesus. This is indicated in the distinction between the "casting out" of evil spirits and the "curing" or "healing" of spirits.[5] There is a further contrast between "evil" spirits and "unclean" spirits.[6] Given that all emotional and mental illnesses were attributed to such spirits, the contrast of the terminology indicates more than one ministry. In Luke we find "some women who had been cured of evil spirits and maladies" (Lu. 8:2) and also "those who were troubled with unclean spirits were cured" (Lu. 6:18; see also Lu. 7:21). In contrast we note many passages where the evil spirits were cast out by Jesus or being discussed as about to be cast out (See Matthew 8:16, 8:31, 9:33, 17:18 et sq, Mk. 9:17, Lu. 9:40, 11:14).

Professor Kelsey develops an excellent presentation on the understanding that the healing of the Lord included inner healing. Professor Kelsey demonstrates that only with modern psychiatry and psychology did man realize the dimensions of emotional illness. He shows that not until the twentieth century did medical science develop the psychotherapeutic understanding of the emotional and mental basis of sickness independent of causal physical damage or evil spirits. He also analyzes the work of Dr. Carl Jung and concludes:

> "As Jung stressed again and again it was not he as psychiatrist who achieved the healing of a sick person. His task was rather to bring the individual to a source of healing found within the psyche, yet which seemed to come from outside it, like a spring bubbling up into a little pond."[7]

With this understanding we can see that what the evangelists had to express in the two categories of physical healing and deliverance or exorcism really contained the third category of inner healing. The Lord healed and freed but the Church, and in particular the evangelists, could only express the events in the language and categories available to them. The Holy Spirit inspired the words of the Gospels but except for rare direct quotations of the Lord's statements, the words of the Gospels are words of men. Modern psychiatry has proven the validity of psychiatric healing. Is it not silly to contend that Jesus healed all forms of physical diseases but did not heal the very real diseases of the inner man? Indeed, the tendency of theologians is to presume that most of the exorcisms of Jesus were psychiatric healings rather than deliverances from evil spirits. Therefore, whether the inner healing is to be found in the exorcism events or under such phrases as "all kinds of sickness and disease" (Mt. 4:23) or "every sickness and every disease" (Mt. 9:35), clearly inner healings are included in the ministry of Jesus.

In the healing of the paralytic, we have both an inner and physical healing (Lu. 5:17-26). First, the Lord restored peace to the inner man by forgiving his sins. This healing gave him the freedom to receive a fullness of physical life, where his paralysis had been both real and symptomatic of his inner bondage. The man "went home praising God" exhibiting his internal freedom to praise and his acknowledgment of the external healing.

When the Lord told Peter of his coming denial he stated ". . . I have prayed for you and once you have recovered, you in your turn must strengthen your brothers" (Lu. 22-31-34). Was not this prayer that the healing love of God would overcome the guilt and shame that Peter would experience so that Peter would be internally strong to strengthen his brothers? Does not the teaching of the Lord that our body should "be fully illumined as when a lamp shines brightly for you" (Lu. 11:33-36) give us a visual image of an inner healing? It contrasts with the suppressing of painful and terrifying events into the darkness of our minds and thus we fail "to take care our light is not darkness."[8]

These passages of scripture have taken on deep meaning for us because our experience is that the same healing is available to us today. We have experienced inner healing occurring more frequently after prayer than physical healing. We have also experienced a phenomenon that will not surprise anyone in the counselling or healing professions: many physical diseases disappear after a person has received an inner healing. There is a mysterious dimension of our lives which integrates the inner and outer man to an extent far beyond what we all recognize to be the psychosomatic.

Once again, we refer here to our experience of healings and not miracles. We do not have demonstrable evidence that the only explanation for the healing was the direct action of God. What we have are beautiful striking experiences in which we prayed for the Lord's action, we believed in the Lord's presence and we observed significant improvement that seemed directly related to the Lord's power. We have prayed for two married women who underwent extensive psychiatric treatment to the point where the various doctors told them they could give no hope for improvement. Both had to cease any employment and were at the point of being committed to a mental institution. After prayer both improved significantly and now are working and living in happier homes. Both still are suffering from some anxiety.

We have prayed for women who hated men, men who rebelled against all authority figures in their life, men and women who were convinced they were unlovable and acted that way, men and women who couldn't place trust in anyone else, alcoholics, dope addicts, schizophrenics, those whose lives were substantially impaired by fears of darkness, being alone, failure, sex, and most commonly those with dominating feelings of guilt and inferiority. In every case where there was a series of contacts there has been improvement. In each category mentioned there has been a person substantially or fully healed as best we can determine.

We have listened to people witness to how the Lord healed them from various problems of inner sickness. We do not include these here because they lack the specificity that is present when there is a special time of prayer for a specific person and the results are confirmed both by the person and those ministering in prayer. Also, our topic here specifically concerns ministering inner healing; the actions of others who lead a prayer for healing.

## MINISTERING

The use of the term "ministering" is to further define our subject as that which involves intercessory prayer. Intercessory prayer is the prayer of one person on behalf of another person. It is the prayer to God seeking some benefit for another party. It is frequently stated that a person can minister to himself and there is truth in this. Nevertheless, this would more properly be called prayer of petition within the direct relationship of man to God. Many principles of ministering inner healing can be applied within the direct prayer of a person for his own healing but we do not attempt here to analyze the mysterious subjective developments within an individual's prayer life. We speak instead of the New Testament ministry as formed in the Gospels and Epistles.

The Lord commissioned his disciples to "heal." The

evangelists recount various times when the Lord commissioned both the twelve and his disciples to "heal the sick," "cure diseases," "lay hands on the sick" (Mt. 10:7-8, Luke 10:8-9, Mark 16:17-18). Saint Paul refers to this ministry in 1 Cor. 12:9 "through the Spirit one receives faith; by the same Spirit another is given the gift of healing"; the Acts of the Apostles records eight individual healings by the apostles.[9]

To minister is to serve and in our context to perform a service of the Lord for others. Specifically here we are referring to healing done by the Lord Jesus through the power of his Spirit. We minister by helping the person seeking healing to be in a right relationship to the Lord, to receive healing and then to participate in intercessory prayers for the healings. Our experience in ministering is that each healing has followed some unique aspect in the approach. Some healings have come through prayer at the end of counselling sessions. Healings of areas which are the roots of habitual sinfulness have most frequently come in a confessional situation. Healings of areas at the root of poor personal relationships have frequently come within the context of a Eucharistic Liturgy. Healings of suicidal compulsions have come in connection with anointing and the administration of the sacrament of the sick.

Many of the healings which brought immediate experience of substantial new freedom followed a long session where a team of people prayed and discerned in the areas of repressed memories, the subconscious and the attitudes of the heart. These areas will be discussed at length in Chapter V.

The wounds that need inner healing are not just the wounds of individuals. There are ways in which relationships, communities and societies are wounded that require reconciliation and healing. Certainly there are injustices and specifically oppressions that create pressures to scar people for life. What is the solution? In personal relationships we have found that each party needs to be healed and then the reconciliation and healing needs to be effected for the relationship. This has been successful with married couples. Prayer for the wounds of being used, taken for granted and treated as inadequate is followed for the spouses by prayer for understanding, generosity and unity for the couples. The same approach is followed for households and religious communities. This is the basis of a reconciled and healed society which is based on justice and true peace. Too many times have we had violent men protesting against violence. Too many times have we had self-pitying men demonstrating for generous care and compassion. Our communities desperately need justice, non-violence and self-giving love but they can only be led to it by those who have it in themselves.

So, when we speak in this chapter of *the ministry of inner healing*, we mean intercessory prayer seeking health in the inner being of a person who is present and is seeking such healing. This chapter began with the celebrated passage from the fifth chapter of the Epistle of Saint James. Verse 13 of the chapter states: "If anyone among you is suffering hardship, he must pray." This apparently means direct prayer to God for relief. In the next verse he who is sick is told to ask others for prayer and it is the prayer in verse 15 that "will reclaim the one who is ill." Therefore if it is a matter of illness, intercessory prayer is the prescription for healing. This is not just a matter of physical sickness since the internal state of sin is joined with it: "declare your sins to one another and pray for one another that you may find healing" (v. 16). The presbyters of the Church are designated "to pray over him anointing him with oil in the name of the Lord," but no restrictions are placed on the intecessory prayer in verse 16: "pray for one another, that you may find healing."

We are all called to some form of the ministry of inner healing; the presbyters and their successors are called to a specific form representing the Church and using the anointing of the Church. But all are called to minister in the "name of the Lord" so that "the Lord will restore him to health."

The common questions regarding this ministry are: what needs to be healed; who should pray for a healing; when should we pray; how should we pray; how much should we expect; and how much preparation and initiative should come from the person to be healed?

These and other questions can only be answered if we understand the goal of inner healing. This is not a situation where man decides what he wants and goes out and gets it. Frequently, people have others pray for them for tranquility, calmness, stability, understanding, tolerance, joy, freedom from anxiety, resentments or guilt but nothing appears to happen. People are naturally inclined to seek after such desirable goods the way they would academic degrees, business success or physical development with the one additional point that they seek through God rather than other men. This is not the way to inner healing by the Lord.

The Lord has his gift for us and we must adjust to accepting his gift. We don't determine what we want and how we will attain it. We decide to accept the Lord's gift and to do whatever is necessary so that we will receive and retain it. We look to him for directions. At the same time, we are not passive but need actively to accept and stand in faith believing that healing is given to us. For that healing the resulting health is the promised gift: the peace of Jesus Christ.

# II
# The Peace of Jesus Christ

"Peace is my farewell to you, my peace is my gift to
you; I do not give it to you as the world gives peace"
(John 14:27).

The peace of Jesus Christ is a distinct gift from the
Lord; it is different from those things given by the world
under the name of peace. It is real; it can be clearly discerned and easily distinguished from what is not the
Lord's gift. Therefore, we understand the process of inner
healing to the extent that we understand this peace. Only
if we know what we are seeking and the extent to which it
is lacking can we know how to begin our ministry of
prayer. And only if we can recognize that healing is happening can we know what to seek next. But we will not
recognize that healing if we do not recognize the peace of
Jesus which is the fullness of that healing.

## SIGNS OF THE PEACE OF JESUS

We recognize the peace of Jesus by many signs. St.
Paul exhorts the Philippians: "Rejoice in the Lord always!
I say it again, rejoice! Everyone should see how unselfish
you are. The Lord is near. Dismiss all anxiety from your

minds. Present your needs to God in every form of prayer
and in petitions full of gratitude. Then God's own peace,
which is beyond all understanding, will stand guard over
your hearts and minds in Christ Jesus" (Philippians 4:4).

We immediately know some characteristics of the
peace of Jesus. It is a peace in which the person always
rejoices. How little most Christians rejoice! They don't
see an occasion to rejoice. They look at outward events
and decide the events are discouraging and depressing:
bad news. They decide they will rejoice if things ever get
better or when they can escape from reality through par-
tying or fantasy. But even then they know it will not be
real joy.

The peace of Jesus involves real joy because of the
gift within us. It does not depend on this or that event. It
is not disrupted by war, political corruption, confusion in
the Church, loss of business, sickness and death of family
or even the prevalence of injustice and oppression in the
world. It is based on the reality of a presence—the reality
of the Spirit of Jesus Christ which Spirit has overcome the
world.

It is a peace by which "everyone sees how unselfish
we are." People do not see all we have acquired, how successful we were in business competition or how we ac-
cumulated the best goods of the world. They see how "unselfish we are" because we are willing to give all that away.
Our security is in a gift: the new presence of Jesus!

It is a peace in which "we dismiss all anxieties from
our minds." We are not anxiously seeking what we do not
have nor are we anxiously protecting what we do have.
We are at rest, tranquil in what we have and that it will
remain.

It is a peace in which are presented all "needs to God

in every form of prayer." Because of what we have, we confidently present all needs, not fearing that we might be asking too much. And our petitions are "full of gratitude," thanking God for all we have received and what we know confidently we will receive.

It is a peace that will "stand guard over your hearts and minds in Christ Jesus." It is a peace that protects our hearts and minds from attack. It enables our life to be hidden in God with Christ Jesus (Colossians 3:3). This means that we cannot be overcome by any force of the world. Our life is safe in God. No matter what forces of evil or rejection by men come upon us in our apostolic service, we cannot be overcome as long as our life is in God through the peace of Christ.

In the next lines of his letter to the Philippians, St. Paul develops the qualities of the man of peace.

"Finally, my brothers, your thoughts should be wholly directed to that which is true, all that deserves respect, all that is honest, pure, admirable, decent, virtuous or worthy of praise. Live according to what you have learned and accepted, what you have heard me say and do. Then will the God of peace be with you" (Philippians 4:8-9).

How simple but crucial. "Be wholly directed to that which is true": no falsity, no make-believe, no pressing the Spirit to state as true what we only hope is true. Finally, Saint Paul teaches that the man living in the peace of Jesus will have the openness to respect and reverence the good in all about him. For Saint Paul peace is a rhythm of being and a way of living and relating, not a particular object to be sought and striven after.

The peace of Christ is that peace which yields the

fruits of the Spirit: "love, joy, peace, patient endurance, kindness, generosity, faith, mildness and chastity" (Galatians 5:22). It is a peace in which we crucify the "flesh with its passions and desires" (Galatians 5:24). These passions and desires are detailed by Saint Paul as what proceeds from unredeemed flesh: "lewd conduct, impurity, licentiousness, idolatry, sorcery, hostilities, bickering, jealousy, outbursts of rage, selfish rivalries, dissensions, factions, envy, drunkenness, orgies and the like" (Galatians 5:20).

The above do not exhaust the characteristic signs of the presence of the peace of Jesus. They do show the nature of the peace and, therefore, what is to be renounced and what is to be embraced by one who would receive this peace. Many come for inner healing but are unwilling to forgive an injury or forget a resentment. They wish to have peace and still nurture the wrongs against them. Or they want the peace of Christ without having the love, generosity and self-sacrifice of Christ. It isn't possible and it doesn't happen. Men and women cannot retain jealousies and rivalries and competitive spirits and have the peace of Jesus Christ. These must be renounced and the opposite embraced. Many come in the name of love to have the peace of Jesus while retaining patterns of impurity and selfishness. It can't be done.

## THE PEACE OF THE WORLD

This peace of Jesus Christ is a distinct peace from the peace of the world. How quickly the "masters of the world" will urge people to deny themselves nothing, fulfill all desires, and release all passions. How facilely they will urge people "to be self-actualized" without concern for what is self-actualized. Aggression, fornication, blasphemy, lying and obtaining what one wants at all costs are only too frequently propounded in popular books as the paths to peace. That peace has nothing to do with the peace of Jesus.

There is another form of worldly peace which appears good but ultimately leads to frustration and desperation. Paul Tournier, a Christian psychologist, describes this peace of achievement. Man is constantly in search of his "place" which will yield peace in his life. Because of his cultural environment, he easily assumes that peace can only be attained by climbing a ladder of achievement.[10] His climb is filled with anxiety, compulsively moving toward that rung in the ladder where he will have everything, have it "all together." He seeks that rung where he will have emerged from the crowd, triumphed over all obstacles and anyone in his way to his place of peace. This is the concept of the book, *An American Tragedy*, and the subsequent movie, *A Place in the Sun*, in which the hero wills the death of his mistress so that he might arrive at his place of peace. This is also the theme of the current popular work, *Hope For The Flowers,*[11] where people are depicted as caterpillars who climb over one another in desperate attempts to reach the top of the pile only to find after exhausting efforts and oppressive violence to others that there is nothing at the top of the pile. It has been a climb to nowhere. True peace comes in being changed by God from a caterpillar to a butterfly and this only happens to those who stop struggling up the ladder and respond confidently in God's plan for them.

There are other forms of peace which are good in themselves and help many people but which fall distinctly short of the peace of Jesus. There are forms of peace called truce, arbitration and compromise. These bring cessation to hostilities but they do not bring right order and inner peace. There are contracts and barters on 50-50 plans which leave the parties 50% at peace. There are forms of peace based on knowing your problems and living with them and knowing your violent feelings and handling them. There are systems of knowing yourself through understanding your id, ego and superego[12] or understanding your parent, child and adult.[13] These understandings which enable a person to know the truth in himself and enable him to know which voices to ignore and which to follow can bring new mental health, but they cannot achieve the peace of Jesus. It is important to believe "I'm OK" but it isn't the fullness of the peace the Lord has for us. For the most part, these systems see the past as containing necessary evils to be handled and adjusted to.

We cannot stop at this point, for we believe that the peace of Jesus views the past as falling in the domain of the lordship of Christ and therefore subject to his salvation and healing. This peace can only be based on a new ordering of our lives, a transformation of our past as well as our present. It is unlimited in its hope and responds affirmatively to Saint Paul's declaration "This means that if anyone is in Christ, he is a new creation. The old order has passed away; now all is new" (2 Corinthians 5:17). How overwhelming is the concept of a new creation! We are not just remodeled or overhauled; we are new to the greatest extent imaginable to man—to the point of creation: something made from nothing. And our ministry of inner healing finds basis in the following line: "all this has been done by God, who has reconciled us to himself through Christ and has given us the ministry of reconciliation" (2 Cor. 5:18). We are called to partake of that radical process described by Saint Paul: "what you have done is put aside your old self with its past deeds and put on a new man, one who grows in knowledge as he is formed anew in the image of his creator (Colossians 3:9-10). Thus, he urges the Romans: "be transformed by the renewal of your mind" (Romans 12:2).

## FOUNDATION OF THE PEACE OF JESUS

What, then, is the root or focal point of this peace? It is the peace of Jesus and we need not be surprised that it rests on Jesus being the center of our lives. It is the peace based on the traditional theological definition of peace as tranquility in order. There must be that justice, that truth, that right order that puts all things in correct perspective and yields the tranquility which is the fruit of the Spirit. It is based on a new presence of Jesus through his Spirit at the center of our lives. The presence of his Spirit is a dimension not just qualitatively better than what we had before but absolutely better than any improvement we could bring about in ourselves. That Spirit is the new ingredient which makes the peace "not like the world gives peace." And it is this Spirit which belongs to Jesus and the Father, which we cannot control, that determines the ingredients of the peace. We can only accept and cooperate with the Spirit of Jesus, inviting the Spirit into every area of our life or we can reject and deny the Spirit. But, we cannot control who the Spirit of Jesus is or how he convicts or where he presses for our response. It is in yielding to this Spirit that we find the peace of Jesus.

The Spirit of Jesus is restless that our lives be in right order to Jesus as Lord and brother, to God as Father and to all men as brothers and sisters. It is restless to reconcile our lives with God and man. The Spirit reveals Jesus to us as risen Lord and present and reveals to us our place in the body of Jesus and our right and grace filled relationship to all men and women in accord with their right relationship to Jesus. The Spirit reveals the Father as Abba, "Dad," "dear Father," a personal intimate loving father. He is a father who has called each of us by name, who has numbered the hairs of our head, who knows our needs before we ask, who has given us a kingdom and who adopts us to stand in the place of Jesus as sons. It is to the extent that we respond and take our place in the footprints of Jesus, accepting the whole truth of that place from the cross to the glory of the risen life, that we will know this gift of peace. We are not appendages of God's family; we are not second class adopted sons; we are truly in the place of the Son of God incorporated into the life process of the Trinity. The love of the Father for the Son passes through our very being and the Son's serving and glorifying the Father passes through us in like manner. We have been grasped by Jesus and interposed into the life of God's family.

Because the Spirit of Jesus and therefore the life of Jesus himself is at the very core of our being, this Spirit presses us to relationships of love, compassion and outreach to all men, particularly the poor and oppressed. We find a new freedom in serving those whom formerly we avoided.

It is important to see this order with the Spirit of Jesus as central. We can appreciate the order and rhythm in a concert orchestra, in a military parade, in a highly trained football team. The orchestra follows the lead of the conductor who establishes all cues and places every member of the orchestra in relationship to himself. The military parade can only begin if everyone first falls into rank based on one man. A football team can only line up in offensive formation if everyone sets himself in relationship to the center who holds the ball. These are examples of right order. How much more must our life be formed on Christ, centered on him and conducted by his direction.

The Spirit, which is a spirit of truth, presses us to confront all the evils of our life and the world about us. We are not embarrassed by any evil but cry with Jesus: I have come for sinners; I have come to save, not to judge. We particularly are called to confront the evils in our present and past life. We are to see the truth in these areas but be confident that we are conquerors with Jesus who triumphed over all sin and death; we can face any rejection, any oppression, any horror, any experience of unlove in our lives. We know that the wounds from these experiences can be healed and that the peace of Jesus can be experienced in the very memories we have of these events. We know these memories are healed when we experience the fruits of the Spirit, the fruits of the peace of Jesus, when we recall the memories—"love, joy, peace, patient endurance, kindness, generosity, faith, mildness and chastity" (Galatians 5:22)—where formerly we knew feelings of oppression, binding, shame, cowardice, resentment, despair and the like.

## THE HEALING PROCESS UNTO
## THE PEACE OF JESUS

The following is a helpful illustration of the wounding and healing process. We have all observed at some time the crying of a hurt little child. The child walking on a sidewalk, in a department store, or in a supermarket is momentarily separated from his mother, trips and falls. The child cries out in fright and hurt. If the mother is at his side she will stoop down and pick him up. She will hold him and say all is well, will caress him and love him. Immediately, the love of the mother for the child becomes more powerful than the anguish, the surprise, the traumatic experience. The child's feeling of being alone and hurt, the effects of the fall become healed. But if the mother is not close, if they've wandered a distance apart, then the child starts a deep cry. We all know how hysteria can take over in those circumstances. And the child screams within himself: "I'm all alone," "I'm hurting," "Nobody cares." When the mother finally comes to the child, she has something more serious to handle. Have you ever noticed a mother can come and pick up a child and the child seemingly cannot even recognize the mother because he is so hysterical? The wound is already going deep within the being; it takes a great deal of talking, of working through the event, in order that such an experience doesn't continue to be frightening in the child's life.

All of us have had experiences like that from earliest childhood. We've had times when we have felt abandoned by our families, unloved by our father and mother, rejected by friends, betrayed by those we put our trust in, unjustly abused and punished; we felt as if we were all alone in the world and that world was in pieces. If there had been sufficient love present to us at those times, we would have been healed. But there wasn't. In each of our lives, there are these areas of unlove, memories which we can't continue to look at because they are so horrifying. We suppress them, we package them, we put them in closets down within ourselves and say, "I'm going to close that closet door and not look at them."

What happens when we come to know the Spirit of Jesus Christ within us, when we have experienced the release of that Spirit, or however we experience the power of Jesus as real in our lives is that we have a new dimension within us. We then know in the present that we are loved, or we know something similar. We know a new experience of salvation, a new experience of being cared for, of being grasped, of being picked up by the Lord; we have a new sense of his presence in our life. And that experience can indeed be the key we can use to open those closed doors and have those memories of the past meet the experiences of the present. We can have the love of Jesus Christ we know today meet and come together with the experience of a time when we thought no one, anywhere, loved us. Now we know Christ loves us; not just loves us but has loved us from the beginning, and was present even at that time when we thought we were alone. He is not just present, but present with the power over any anxiety, over any evil in our lives, through his love. When those experiences come together, then Jesus becomes a living reality in that memory. Instead of seeing this memory as only a tripping and falling on our face, we become like the child who sees in his memory the love of his mother. We see the love of Jesus and the love of God our Father for us in that memory. We know that love is real and we can experience, right in that scene, the same love we experience in our present life with God.

This peace of Jesus Christ is the substance of inner healing. It is necessary to retain a clear idea of this peace to discern the process of inner healing in any life. There are so many ways in which healing unto new peace in general and the peace of Christ in particular can take place. It is helpful to categorize stages and procedures in order that the ministry may be clear. This is not to contend that the Lord only acts in this way. It is rather to show the normal development and then urge the reader to be watchful for the creativity of the ever new Spirit.

The healing contact between the memory world of unlove and the present experience of salvation and love through the Lordship of Jesus comes in different forms. Sometimes a recent memory of rejection is the object of healing; sometimes it is a hidden repressed memory of early life; sometimes it is a series of memories; sometimes it is a pattern of life that continues almost independently of any memories. At times, healing comes because a person has let go of wounds he was nurturing and using for escaping reality, justifying failure or gaining attention and affection: he commits himself to Jesus and lets go of other things to grasp a new reality in his life. At times, he desires to make this commitment, but he is prevented from doing it by those bound-up areas of his life. He may be bound by resentments in which he hasn't decided to forgive. He may be bound by the presence of evil which has not been subjected to the authority of Jesus Christ. All these variables illustrate the importance of the minister of inner healing who can speak the needed words of truth and love.

# III
# The Minister of
# Inner Healing

"All this has been done by God, who has reconciled us to himself through Christ and has given us the ministry of reconciliation. I mean that God in Christ was reconciling the world to himself, not counting men's transgressions against them, and that he has entrusted the message of reconciliation to us. This makes us ambassadors for Christ, God, as it were, appealing through us" (2 Cor. 5:18-21).

We are called to be ministers of reconciliation. That reconciliation finds its completion in the peace of Jesus Christ. We have his message of good news—he is saviour; he brings freedom; he gives us his Spirit and his peace. But, we need to know how to reach out to our brother and sister who are lacking this peace.

## THE ROLE OF MINISTER

The answer is simple but not easy. We reach out with the heart of Jesus. They experience in us the love of Jesus desiring their freedom. This will become clearer if we detail what we are not called to be and what approach we are called to follow.

We are not called to become saviours or to be perfect models of peace. Jesus, the Lord alone, is the Saviour and the model of peace. We are as Henri Nouwen so beautifully developed it, wounded healers.[14] We are scarred and damaged by so much unlove in our own lives that it would be a violation of truth to represent a condition of perfection. Indeed, our very power as ministers rests on our weakness and sinfulness. We can understand the bound state of others because we have been bound by our own sins and the sins of others. We can live in ourselves what the other is experiencing, because our experience is not that different. Further, we are part of the sin of all men. This person's sufferings are related to our own sinfulness. He is part of what I have done and part of the body in which I live. If I had been more loving, less sinful, more absorbing of the world's violence, more filled with the peace of Jesus, might not his condition be better? Our woundedness identifies us with all others who are wounded; and yet this very weakness becomes our strength. In weakness we make contact with our brother; if we were strong unto perfection, how would the contact be made? We would appear as superior and separate. And more, as Saint Paul writes: "when I am powerless it is then that I am strong" (2 Cor. 12:10). Because we recognize our weakness, we can dismiss any efforts to rely on our strength and turn to the true strength from the Lord. The minister, then, is called to proclaim the close relationship between himself and the one seeking healing, who thereby will realize that he is not alone and is not a different class Christian. He is among his own. He and the minister have a common Father, a common Saviour and the same Lord. The minister will come to realize that the healing he is praying for is in a true sense his own, because he is part of the same body as the person seeking healing.

The minister should not allow the peace of Jesus to be understood as a burden. It is a gift—a free gift—not to be earned, not to be offered to some and denied to others. The person seeking healing will frequently feel he is unworthy and that he could never live up to the requirements of the gift. The minister must proclaim the nature of the gift and the need to be willing to receive it in all its aspects. But, his ministering is true service when he reflects that he has known this peace as a free gift in his life —a gift not impeded by his unworthiness.

The minister cannot love with his love alone; it is not enough. His brother needs to know he is loved by Jesus. The minister should ask to know the love of Jesus for his brother and to transmit this love. He asks that the love of Jesus infill and direct his own love so that there is a fulness of love expressed in accord with the right relationship between the parties. The love is both human and divine. It is incarnate love reaching out to the person. It is revealing to note that Morton Kelsey cites Bruno Klopfer, the authority on the Rorschach test, as stating that 50% of all psychic therapy consists of warm practical concern.[15] The freedom to relate in a warm loving way will come to the extent the minister comprehends the ongoing love of the Lord for both himself and the one seeking healing.

The minister should never see himself as alone in his work of the Lord. In fact, whenever possible, he should not be alone with the person. Two or more gathered in the name of Jesus brings a special presence of Jesus. It better represents the Body of Jesus and prevents the minister from appropriating the glory to himself. It also multiplies the gifts and ministries that are available. The ministering team is fortified by charismatic gifts of faith, love, discernment of spirits, words of wisdom and knowledge, and prophecy, as well as gifts of compassion, understanding and piety. Even where the minister is forced to be alone because of a sacramental confession, extreme confidentiality of matter, or urgency of time, the minister should consciously identify himself as representing the Body of Christ and where possible seek prayer support. Ideally, the healing will take place in the healing environment of a community of love. This ideal is still so rare that for now we will confine ourselves to the less desirable but more common situations.

The minister should not rely just on his analysis nor on hypotheses; he should expect that what he needs to know and needs to do will be revealed to him. This revelation can come in many forms from natural and supernatural sources but it should have a sign of confirmation by the Lord. Sometimes the person states the problem, its source and the needed prayer. The minister knows a peace and confidence in his spirit that moves him to confirm and begin prayer. Sometimes there is lengthy discernment involving narrations, testing of spirits (whether what is being said comes from the Holy Spirit, the human spirit or an evil spirit), specific revelations through words of wisdom and knowledge, or the revealing of the secret of the heart explained by Saint Paul in 1 Cor. 14:25. There is an interplay among the ministers and their brother and there ordinarily should be confirmation through the affirming action of the Spirit before beginning a prayer for healing. This affirmation of the Spirit has the scriptural signs of light, building up the body, peace, an outreach of love and the fruits of the Spirit specified in Galatians 5:22.

The minister should not act in his own name but rely explicitly and implicitly on the name of Jesus. He should be careful that Jesus is the beginning and end of the discernment and prayer session, that is, that the direction and power be sought from the Lord for the purpose of bringing the person in union with the Lord through the gift of his peace.

## THE APPROACH OF THE MINISTER

The minister who seeks to serve with the heart of Jesus—as a wounded and healed sinner, celebrating the gift of the peace of Christ, relying on the love of Jesus to work through him, and acting in the name of Jesus in conjunction with other members of the Body—will thereby follow certain general patterns. His approach will be one of affirmation in love and truth; he will therefore always reflect an affirmation of and a love for the true good that is in the person.[16] He will always be good news more than bad news. Only if his brother knows this affirmation of greater good will he be able to face the evil, sinfulness, and weakness of his life. This affirmation takes many forms; initially it is manifested through an environment of loving acceptance, explicit acknowledgment of the good and gifts of his brother and reflecting back expressed ideas and feelings.[17] It is especially important that the person know that it is all right to have negative feelings. Feelings in themselves are neither right nor wrong; it is only how we respond to our feelings that creates the moral or immoral behaviour. We have experienced people in deep despair over suicidal, hate and sexual feelings. When the person hears that he can still be faithful to God and man while having such feelings, he frequently relaxes and the source of the problem is eliminated through the inner healing or deliverance ministry.

Affirmation is manifested through a spirit of praise. While remaining sensitive to the level of faith of the subject, the minister should lead and encourage a spirit that praises God in all things. The minister might gently witness to how God has worked in his life to bring good out of apparently undesirable events. "God makes all things work together for the good of those who have been called according to his decree" (Rom. 8:28). The subject should hear the good news that there is no situation, no condition, no event, in which God's power of goodness cannot overcome the evil. Truly the Christian praises God in every situation and praises him that his love and goodness can triumph in every event of one's life. Merlin Carothers has written two excellent books on the place of praise in the Christian life: *From Prison to Praise* and *Power in Praise.*[18]

This good news approach of affirmation should rely on the Good News: the Gospels and all scriptures. It is in scripture that we find the words of power to change lives. The scriptures breathe the power of the Holy Spirit and can accomplish infinitely more than our own words. The words of scripture when properly applied will reveal, convict, encourage, heal and direct. We have seen the following scripture passages properly applied to affect profoundly people's lives: "Fear not little flock; it has pleased the Father to give you a kingdom" (Lu. 12:32); "I did not come to condemn the world but to save it" (Jn. 12:47); "By his wounds you were healed" (1 Pt. 2:24); "Leave your gift at the altar; go first to be reconciled with your brother" (Mk. 5:24); "How much more will the Father give the Holy Spirit to those who ask him" (Lu. 11:14); "Those who were troubled with unclean spirits were cured: indeed the whole crowd was trying to touch him because power went out from him which cured all" (Lu. 6:18).

## AUTHORITY OF THE MINISTER

The approach of the minister should rest firmly on the authority of Jesus. This means that he should be confident of the truth and power of the word of scripture. This means he should be confident that the Lord loves the persons needing healing, that the Lord wills that the power of healing be at the service of love, and, therefore, that whenever healing is the most loving thing for the person within the whole Body, the Lord wills the healing. Finally, the minister should be confident that ordinarily the Lord wills to work through him to bring healing to others. "Signs like these will accompany those who have professed their faith: they will use my name to expel demons, they will speak entirely new languages, they will be able to handle serpents, they will be able to drink deadly poison without harm and the sick upon whom they lay their hands will recover" (Mk. 16:17-19).

In the case of healing, the minister uses the faith he truthfully has as fully as possible. His faith in the will and power of Jesus to heal at the specific moment should be proclaimed as clearly as possible. He is acting in the name of Jesus; Jesus is the healer. But, Jesus has willed his power to the Church and depends on his ministers using that power in faith. We do not have the ministering of healing as our own ministry but as belonging to the Lord. We cannot use the ministry to bring healing where and when we want it, but we can use it to effect healing as the Lord leads us through his Spirit. When we conclude through discernment that this is the time and place to pray for a healing, we should use all the authority our faith allows us.

The minister should come against evil with authority. Persons are not only bound by the internal wounds of the past but at times by the more direct action of the forces of evil. This is an area of authority integrally related to the healing ministry. Freeing our brothers of binding evil in their lives must precede at times such prayers for healing as previously discussed.

The use of authority in this manner is broadly called exorcism or deliverance. Exorcism in the formal sense involves a designated priest or minister employing a prescribed rite authorized by Church authority. For Roman Catholics, The Roman Ritual has such a rite.[19] This formal exorcism rite is intended to free those who in the strict sense are possessed; that is, despite retaining their free will, they are substantially controlled by evil spirits which seriously impede the exercise of that will.[20]

The second area of authority is that of coming against evil which is in some way binding the person. Many times there is a wall-like separation between the minister and the person. He doesn't know if the basic condition is deep resentment and lack of forgiveness, deep overpowering inner wounds, or the presence of evil spirits. There may be a pattern of fear, dumbness or scrupulosity. We proclaim the saving power of Jesus, his love for the person, his Spirit given to us. And we use the authority of the name of Jesus to break the hold of what is not of God.

At times, there is an oppression of evil that needs only to be rebuked in the name of Jesus. Other times, the person appears so tied into his condition that he cannot respond. In such cases it is helpful for the minister to use visual terms to express what is happening. He can picture the black wall enclosing him and the light of Jesus piercing this darkness, breaking it into pieces and gradually overcoming it. This visualization enables the person to co-operate with what is in fact happening. He recognizes the binding darkness of what is not of God in his life. He recognizes his inability to break this darkness. He accepts Christ as the light which can pierce these bonds. He relates to the faith of the minister who believes in the presence and power of this light. He responds to the words of John 1:45, "whatever came to be in him, found life, life for the light of men. The light shines on in darkness, a darkness that did not overcome it."

The third area of authority is that of deliverance, also known as informal exorcism.[21] This book attempts to treat in depth the ministry of inner healing. The deliverance ministry requires a similar development which is beyond the scope of our subject. Nevertheless, we acknowledge here the true place of deliverance in the Lord's plan to bring freedom into our lives, and we make what pertinent reflections seem necessary for the effectiveness of the minister of inner healing. Deliverance ministry, even more than inner healing ministry, requires a body or team approach. It requires a period of discernment to test carefully the spirits as to whether the source of the block is of man or evil. It requires preparation of the ministers and the person. The ministers give themselves to prayerful preparation so that they will be open and sensitive to the Lord's leading. The individual repents of sinfulness, renounces all evil, decides to forgive all injuries, and, to the extent possible, proclaims Jesus as personal Lord and Saviour. Confidentiality and deep reverence for the person should be observed. All present pray for protection. The ministers seek to identify the binding spirit through a variety of means that include commanding the spirit to identify itself. Once the spirit is identified, the person is asked to renounce it and the minister commands its departure in the name of Jesus as Lord. The process may be short or long in duration, but it is culminated frequently by some distinct sign and always by a new sense of peace in the Lord. When there is confirmation by the minister and the person of the deliverance, they praise and thank the Lord and pray for a healing and infilling of the Holy Spirit for all wounds and disorders occasioned by the presence of evil.

This chapter concerns the role of the minister but brief reference should be made here to the need of the person to use authority. He cooperates in ordering the departure of the evil spirit. After the deliverance, he takes authority in the name of Jesus proclaiming his freedom and rebuking any return of evil. He stands on the authority of the words of scripture that Jesus has totally conquered all evil.

Some readers may find this treatment of deliverance uncomfortable to read. This is understandable. A few years ago, all of us who have teamed in inner healing and deliverance ministries would have had a similar reaction. In the past three years we have experienced the presence of evil in very convincing ways, and, praise God, we have experienced new freedom immediately evidenced in the lives of those who sought deliverance.

At this point, it is fruitful to reflect on the teachings of Pope Paul that one of the greatest needs of the Church today is "defense from the evil which is called the devil." The following excerpts are from the general audience of the Pope on November 15, 1972.

"Evil is not merely a lack of something, but an effective agent, a living spiritual being, perverted and perverting. A terrible reality. Mysterious and frightening.

And how could we forget that Christ, referring three times to the devil as his adversary calls him "prince of this world" (Jn. 12, 31; 14, 30; 16, 11). This overhanging fateful presence is mentioned in many passages of the New Testament. Saint Paul calls him "the God of this world" (1 Cor. 4, 4). He warns us of the struggle in the dark that we Christians must wage not against one Devil only, but against many of them. "Put on the whole armour of God," the Apostle says, "that you may be able to stand against the wiles of the devil. For we are not contending against flesh and blood but against the principalities, against the powers, against the world rulers of this present darkness, against the spiritual hosts of wickedness in the heavenly places" (Eph. 6:11-12).

That it is not a question of one Devil but of many is indicated by various passages in the Gospel (Lk. 11, 21; Mk. 5, 9). But the principal one is Satan, which means the adversary, the enemy; and with him many, all creatures of God, but fallen because of their rebellion and damnation (cf. Denz, Sch. 800-428); a whole mysterious world upset by an unhappy drama, of which we know very little."[22]

A final caution: anyone should be reluctant to take on the ministry of deliverance without the clear call of the Church. The community should call forth mature, knowledgeable people for this ministry. Ideally, the principal minister should have the canonical order of the conferred ministry of exorcist and be approved by the proper bishop for its exercise.

Obviously, this requires learning and formation. The maturity envisioned for the minister specifically means a maturity of character integrated with a proper understanding of the use of the gifts of the Spirit. It is valuable to reflect here on these gifts. In the celebrated passage of Isaiah we read:

> "The Spirit of the Lord shall rest upon him—a spirit of wisdom and of understanding, a spirit of counsel and of strength, a spirit of knowledge and of fear of the Lord, and his delight shall be the fear of the Lord" (Is. 11:2-3).[23]

# IV
# Decision

The most common barrier to the Lord's healing in people's lives is a failure to decide for such healing. People claim they want health and yet hold on to sickness as a rationalization for past and present failures or as a security device to get attention and sympathy. There are others who desire the healing of Christ but have not decided to take Jesus Christ as Saviour and Lord of their lives. Our experience is that many apparently religious and dedicated people have not made these decisions.

Paul Tillich gives us a penetrating analysis of those who cling to their illness and how they are healed through true faith.

"Faith here of course does not mean the belief in assertions for which there is no evidence. It never meant that in genuine religion and it never should be abused in this sense. But faith means being grasped by a power that is greater than we are, a power that shakes us and turns us and transforms us and heals us. Surrender to this power is faith. The people whom Jesus could heal and can heal are those who did and do this self-surrender to the healing power in him. They surrendered their persons, disgusted and despairing about themselves, hateful of themselves and therefore hostile towards everybody else; afraid of life, burdened with guilt feelings, accusing and excusing themselves, fleeing from others into loneliness, fleeing from themselves to others, trying finally to escape from the threats of existence into the painful and deceptive safety of mental and bodily disease. As such beings they surrendered to Jesus and this surrender is what we call faith. But he did not keep them, as a good helper should never do. He gave them back to themselves as new creatures, healed and whole. And when he died he left a group of people who in spite of much anxiety, desire, weakness and guilt had the certitude that they were healed and that the healing power amongst them was great enough to conquer individuals and nations all over the world. We belong to these people if we are grasped by the new reality which has appeared in him. We have his healing power ourselves."[24]

There can be many blocks to deciding for healing but the most common in inner healing is the unwillingness to forgive. Time and again we have counselled and prayed with persons over extended periods and found only minimal improvement. Then we uncover a relationship in which resentment is nurtured and forgiveness is withheld. Frequently, the person is only vaguely aware of the situation. He feels forgiveness is impossible, beyond his resources. And he is right, this is how he *feels* and in terms of freeing him from those feelings, he cannot do it himself. But he can decide for forgiveness. Forgiveness is in the will, in the decision, not in the feelings. When this is explained and the person is told that we are not guilty because of our feelings but only if we respond to our feelings in a wrong way, new freedom comes to make the decision. He responds "I decided to forgive him and I decide to be a forgiving person." The Lord's words again come true "as you measure out to others so it will be measured to you pressed down and running over." The Lord blesses that decision with grace and the person is open to know the Lord's healing. This forgiveness when coupled with confession of sin in the sacrament of penance has proven to be a source of glorious healings. We experience today in forgiveness and healing what the Lord did in forgiving the sins of the paralytic before pronouncing his healing (Luke 5:17-26).

Many people do not accept Jesus as personal saviour in their lives. They hold on to the guilt of their past actions. They believe that such guilt requires them to earn forgiveness over many years. They only accept partial salvation. They are like the prodigal son who thought the best he could do would be a servant in his father's house— until he came home, opened to his father's love and discovered he was truly a son. They have to decide to accept the full salvation the Lord has for them. Sometimes they glory in their past sins, they consider themselves especially important because of the wrong they did in their lives and they hold on to the past and block salvation.

People fail to decide for Jesus as Lord of their lives because they are afraid of facing the future depending only on him. They feel they need their reservedness, their emotional fits, their anxiety routines to use as an escape from reality, present and future. To decide for the Lordship of Jesus is to let go of the future, and to believe that the power of the Lord can triumph over all evil; therefore the continual response of the Christian is to praise the Lord for each day.

To decide for the Lordship of Jesus is to decide to trust. It is to put our security in someone else. This is very frightening for many people. They have never trusted. They have held back in every relationship of their lives.

No one has ever been in the center of their lives; and they pull back from inviting the Lord to that place. Usually, they must experience the Lord's love for them through other men before they can open their lives to invite Jesus to be Lord.

There is another decision that the person must make and this is a confusing one for many. Once he knows that he has been given the faith to accept a healing, that is, to surrender to the Lord's healing power in his life, he must decide for it. Healings given by the Lord are lost because the person does not decide that he is healed. All of us must respond in faith, standing firmly in the faith we have been given, believing ourselves healed when the grace is present. It is a standing, not a wishing; not a vague hoping, not a conditional "if I were open" or "if it be the Lord's will."[25]

This is a very sensitive point with many Christians. It seems to us that the true response to any healing prayer is: I accept the Lord as my healer. I believe with all my heart in that relationship; furthermore, to the fullness of the grace of faith given to me at this moment, I accept the healing in my life. The grace of faith may not be there at times, and, therefore, the healing is not there. The subject must state only what he knows to be true inside himself. It is still the Lord's healing and it cannot be controlled by man desiring healings when they are not given and not confirmed by the grace of faith. To claim a healing without any confirmation in grace is to create two equally bad possibilities. One is that the person, who already has the sickness needing healing, may be made to carry a burden of guilt for not being healed. If on the other hand, the person is not at fault, God must have changed his mind. In the first case, the person's burden has been compounded;

in the second case, God is made to be arbitrary and capricious. Both cases are highly undesirable and therefore the minister should be sensitive not to encourage unwarranted claiming of healing.

This is such a difficult point. We experience people who are prayed with for a healing; they accept the healing in faith, their condition becomes worse for days but they stand on their faith, and they are healed. We also experience people who accept the healing in faith; their condition improves, but not to the extent they desire. So they doubt, turn from the Lord as their healer, and the improvement vanishes. Finally, we experience people, after being prayed with for a healing, who claim the healing and resolutely maintain they have been healed. Their sick condition continues, and, eventually, the person and everyone else recognize that the particular healing has not taken place.

But the truth is that something takes place whenever we turn to the Lord and, calling on the Holy Spirit, ask for a healing; our prayer is heard and a response is given. That response is a gift of love and that gift is directed to our full freedom and health in God forever. But the response may be to convict us of wrong-doing in our life. We may need to right wrong relationships. We may need to forgive or to commit our lives to the Lord. The Lord in love calls us to this rather than giving us at this time the relief from arthritis, allergy, a bad back or even nervousness. Because of our present spiritual circumstances we are better off with the sickness. The sickness is at the moment an instrument of keeping us dependent on God and a healing may mislead the person to believe falsely in his spiritual well-being. With the sickness healed but without the needed spiritual growth, he might give over to vanity and independence from God. Therefore, both ministers and people should be slow to state the particular thing the Lord is doing. We should not proclaim as done something we wish the Lord would do.

We are called to decide for Jesus as saviour, for Jesus as lord and for Jesus as our healer. We are called to decide to forgive, to renounce what is not of God, to accept healing from God and to stand in faith in the healings we have received.

A final word on decision is necessary. As Christians, we are called not just to decide for the healing of our illness but even more to decide for the retention of our health. If our lives are hidden in Christ and Jesus is Lord, then we can stand on that reality against all evil, even sickness. Saint Paul teaches the Christians at Ephesus:

> "There was a time you were in darkness but now you are light in the Lord. Well then, live as children of light. Light produces every kind of goodness and justice and truth" (Eph. 5:8-9).

and later:

> "Finally, draw your strength from the Lord and his mighty power. Put on the armor of God so that you may be able to stand firm against the tactics of the devil" (Eph. 6:10-11).

Many Christians, in our experience, have known new health and vitality because they have stood fast against all evil including all sickness and anxiety. They proclaim with these actions of relying on the Lord's protection and strength that they believe Paul's words:

> "To him whose power now at work in us can do immeasurably more than we ask or imagine—to him be glory in the Church and in Christ Jesus through all generations, world without end. Amen" (Eph. 3:20-21).

# V
# The Process of Healing

We now present the most concrete material we have on methodology. It is difficult to maintain a balance between the dangers of oversystematizing the free actions of the Spirit and failing to utilize the lessons of experience. We find some distinctions to be very important in knowing how to minister the healing power of the Lord.

## CALLING FORTH AND WALKING BACK

The first distinction is between those people whose faith is strong enough to face fully the realities of painful memories and those whose faith and general spiritual well-being is such that reexperiencing past pains is more than they can face. Where the person is conscious of the love of God for him and in faith believes that this love is stronger than any anxiety he might have, then the person can look at painful memories and in faith see himself loved by God at just the time of greatest suffering. The love is stronger than the pain; the result is that the fruits of the Spirit, love, joy, peace and others, can be known in the very memories that formerly brought only fear, guilt and pain. When the faith to believe in this love is not strong enough in relation to the painful memory, then the memory should not be called forth into present consciousness.

There is one very important consideration in applying this standard. Faith is a gift and the Lord frequently gives the necessary faith right at the moment when the person is the subject of the prayer. The minister should always pray first for the person asking for this faith. Only then should he seek the guidance to know whether to call forth specific memories.

If he discerns that the person's faith is not sufficient to face the memory, then the minister should ask the Lord through the power of his Spirit to go back into the past memories and touch them with the healing power of love. The minister might recount the memories from the present back asking the Lord to walk back with his Spirit of healing love and touch each memory with his presence. The minister might pray walking forward from conception when God first called the person's name in love and gave him a share of his life. When there are repressed memories in the unconscious, the power of the Spirit within the person frequently takes the lead and without any vocal prayer by the minister, the person relives those memories that are ready for healing. When the person evidences the presence of anxiety, the minister might ask "where are you now," or "how old are you"? The person will usually answer simply in such words as "I'm eight years old; I'm at home in my room" and then proceed to give details which had apparently been long forgotten. The minister prays the healing love of the Lord into the person laying hands in an appropriate fashion. Usually the person evidences peace and relaxation at which point the minister thanks God for his presence and healing. After a short interlude another memory will arise and the process is repeated.[26]

## SURFACE AND ROOT MEMORIES

The second important distinction is between surface memories and root memories. At times, there is a single memory of an embarrassing act, an incident filled with guilt feelings or a single moment of fright; and this memory can be called forth into the consciousness of the person. The minister prays that the person now experience the love of God in the memory. Following the prayer it is common for the person to experience new peace in the memory.

Where a root memory is involved there are many disturbing memories built upon one root memory. Praying for individual surface memories yields little success. These memories are but parts of the iceberg above the water. There is a reality to be healed beneath the water. When the root is healed, new freedom is experienced in a whole series of other memories. A childhood memory of being alone at night in the dark, being lost amidst a crowd or being unwanted by parents can be the foundation for later fears of darkness, of strangers or of intimacy. Memories of a tyrannical father can be the roots of memories of many subsequent bad authority experiences. At times, the root is so deep and the healing is so radical that the release of new peace and love is an experience comparable or exceeding what is known at the point of the original release of the Spirit called the Baptism of the Spirit.

These deeply rooted memories are frequently healed

with the aid of a visualization process. If the person was frightened at an early age, the minister prays aloud that the person will see Jesus holding her just at that point of fright—that Jesus will be seen now doing the very thing that would have most helped the person at the time of the original incident. We have known persons to visualize Jesus protecting them from some feared danger, Jesus taking them to the Father and introducing them to the first fatherly love they have known, and Jesus taking them to Mary, his mother, and leading them to experience a mother's love. Whatever the true need is, the loving heart of the Lord desires that that need be filled with his saving love; the visualization is but a form of accepting the love the Lord offers.

We have made frequent reference to the healing of father memories. This is because the scars of an unloving father relationship are so much at the root of other problems. Normally children are introduced to God as Father. If "father" means judgment, punishment, distance and abandonment, then the child accepts God as such. Therefore, a lifetime of spiritual activity can be built on a sick foundation. The result is that despite many laudable deeds and desires, fundamentally the person accepts neither that God loves him nor that intimacy and union with God are possible. We have found frequently that a person is in deep rebellion against God while apparently leading a dedicated life for God.

These deep problems of authority and rebellion against God are manifested in patterns of resentment against authority figures, patterns of feeling betrayed by people whom the person once trusted but when they were promoted became unbearable. The priest in the sacrament of penance should be very sensitive to confessions fitting these patterns. If only the current problems are dealt with, then the basic situation will remain unhealed and the series of current problems and sins will continue. How frequently penitents confess for years multiple sins of uncharitableness and impatience with a particular person. Usually the root cause has not been acknowledged or treated. Good resolutions, a firm purpose of amendment and even extended prayer may not help.

## MEMORIES AND HEART

A third distinction is between those inner healings related to specific memories and those that cannot be so directly identified. We have an attitudinal life which operates from the very core of our being. In popular understanding it is a matter of the heart. This life determines broad general patterns of relating to others and relating to God. The *Damn Yankees* song says "you've got to have heart" and we just don't seem to have the heart of loving, giving and sacrificing. Our hearts seem to be of stone or wood. We cannot respond to some people's needs even though our mind tells us it is a good thing to help in the situation. People experience broken-heartedness. And it seems this center of love within is shattered, never again to be the same source of giving and receiving love.

We have experienced the healing of people whose hearts in various degrees appeared to be wounded, hardened or broken. The process of these healings seems to us sufficiently different from the healings of memories to refer to them as healings of the heart. We have also experienced gifts of knowledge to the minister whereby he would know that this type of healing was needed. The minister would speak of the damaged heart and the person would respond with statements of deep confirmation.

Some of the initial manifestations which led to heart healings were a judgemental spirit that is harsh and demanding on self and others, a strong perfectionist attitude demanding the impossible from self and others, a strong pattern of fearing future events, a sense of aloneness and abandonment whenever there are times of decision, a preoccupation with one's own guilt and a compulsive reaction to compete for position and success. These patterns are present in what is otherwise a deeply religious life. Usually there is a constant expectation of growth or breakthrough to new spiritual freedom, but it hasn't happened. It doesn't happen because the heart is hurting.

In a more scientific vein, by heart we mean the volitional and affective centers of one's life. The desires, directions, and attitudes at this level are wrongly centered. We find expression of this in the Epistle of Saint James:

"Where do the conflicts and disputes among you originate? Is it not your inner cravings that make war within your members? What you desire you do not obtain, and so you resort to murder. You envy and you cannot acquire, so you quarrel and fight. You do not obtain because you do not ask. You ask and you do not receive because you ask wrongly, with a view to squandering what you receive on your pleasures. O you unfaithful ones, are you not aware that love of the world is enmity to God? A man is marked out as God's enemy if he chooses to be the world's friend (the unredeemed world subjected to the power of sin). Do you suppose it is to no purpose that Scripture says, "the spirit he has implanted in us tends toward jealousy"? Yet he bestows a greater gift for the sake of which it is written, "God resists the proud but bestows his favor on the lowly." Therefore submit to God; resist the devil and he will take flight. Draw close to God, and he will draw close to you. Cleanse your hands, you sinners; purify your hearts, you backsliders. Begin to lament, to mourn, and to weep; let your laughter be turned into mourning and your joy into sorrow. Be humbled in the sight of the Lord and he will raise you on high" (Ja. 4:1-10).

The biblical authors frequently referred to the heart needing healing and changing. The prophecies of the Old Testament spoke of the new heart Yahweh would give:

"I will give them a new heart and put a new spirit within them. I will remove the stony heart from their bodies and replace it with a natural heart, so they will live according to my statutes and observe and carry out my ordinances; thus they shall be my people and I will be their God!" (Ez. 11:19-20)

The psalmist prays:

"A clean heart create for me O God, and a steadfast spirit renew within me" (Ps. 51:12).

The prophet proclaims:

"The spirit of the Lord God is upon me, because the Lord has anointed me; he has sent me to bring glad tidings to the lowly, to heal the brokenhearted" (Isaiah 61:1).

In the New Testament, the heart is the seat of the divine operations which transform the Christian. The Spirit is sent into the heart (Gal. 4:6), and the love of God is poured into the heart through the Holy Spirit (Rom.

5:5; 2 Cor. 1:22). Christ dwells in the heart (Eph. 3:17). The spirit of wisdom and revelation and the knowledge of Christ Jesus enlightens the eyes of the heart (Eph. 1:17ff). Hardness of heart, on the other hand, is slowness to believe the words of Jesus (Jn. 12:40). In view of what the scriptures indicate concerning the heart, it is not surprising that the healing love of God working in the heart is the dynamic source and center of the healing of the whole person. It seems logical then that all human healing set into action by the renewal grace of Spirit-baptism would eventually move into the heart and mend and heal, and then move out from the "whole heart" through the personality to all the areas and dimensions of a person's existence.

The Lord intends us to know a new heart, a clean heart and a fleshy heart in place of a broken heart, a wounded heart and a hardened heart. This is the Lord's work and in his time we do know it. We have seen this in our lives and those lives to whom we minister. In a moment of grace that appears to be the climax of memory healings, there is a crumbling of the hardened stony heart, or there is a washing clean and new wholeness to the wounded heart, or there is a replacement of the broken heart with the Lord's pastoral heart. We have seen this grace. The person knows the time for a deep inner change is upon him. The minister supports in prayer the good things being done. He reassures the person to persevere through what is frequently a difficult session. The minister intercedes in prayer for the strength of the person in the spiritual and sometimes physical pain of replacing the old heart with the new. This is mystery. The important thing is that the minister knows this is coming, supports it without interfering and prays consolation and peace into the person. The person speaks of knowing a new depth of reconciliation, a new oneness within himself and a oneness with the Body of Jesus. Frequently the person is drawn to the Jesus prayer: "Lord Jesus Christ, Son of the living God, have mercy on me a sinner." The person finds new identity. He realizes that he is part of every man's sin but that he is also part of redemption and new life.

The minister should be open to the gifts which support the action of the Spirit. In wisdom and knowledge the minister can affirm directions and assure the person of the presence of the Lord, but ultimately he is only responding to what the Lord is doing. He is giving loving support, affirming the saving action of God at work. The person himself knows when a new oneness and new peace has come. There is a new ability to pray, a new depth of communication with God, a new sense of identity and resting in that identity, and a new quiet call to holiness. We have found such a healing experience to lead people into the prayer of quiet or to new patterns of prayer with various manifestations of active and passive contemplation. Sometimes the person begins to sense the Lord calling him by name. The healing process of yielding the peace of a new heart can extend over considerable time. Ordinarily there is a time interval of adjustment following the initial transformation experience.

This peak may be accompanied by tears which are also obviously a release unto new peace; and a sense of cracking, crumbling and washing away within the center of a person.

## TRANSPARENCE

Following both root memory and heart healings, there comes a new transparency into the person's life. The

eyes may appear changed. Their demeanor is one of openness before the world, not hiding or maneuvering but a
simple presence. Obviously, the extent to which this happens varies, depending on the spiritual condition of the
person. While this has been our experience, we believe it
should not be used as a test to determine healing.

"You are the light of the world" says the Lord and
indeed this becomes obvious in the case of people so
healed. The prologue of Saint John's Gospel proclaims:

> "In the beginning was the Word; the Word was in
> God's presence and the Word was God. He was
> present to God in the beginning. Through him all
> things came to be. Whatever came to be in him,
> found life, life for the light of men. The light shines
> on in darkness, a darkness that did not overcome it.
> There was a man named John sent by God, who
> came as a witness to testify to the light so that
> through him all men might believe—but only to tes-
> tify to the light, for he himself was not the light. The
> real light which gives light to every man was coming
> into the world" (John 1:1-9).

And Jesus proclaimed:

> "I am the light of the world. No follower of mine
> shall ever walk in darkness; no, he shall possess the
> light of life" (Jn. 8:12).

And we read in the first epistle of John:

> ". . . the commandment that I write you is new, as
> it is realized in him and you, for the darkness is over
> and the real light begins to shine" (1 Jn. 2:8).

These scripture passages proclaim the reality of Jesus as the light of the world. We have found experiential evidence of this truth in observing new light and power in those healed by the Spirit of Jesus. The Spirit shines forth in a new way that evokes from us praise and thanksgiving to our God from whom all light comes.

There are so many unanswered questions at the end of such a presentation or process as this. What is the response to be expected? How much follow-up and support is needed? When can we say a healing is complete? For each person the answer is different. Each relationship with God is unique. The minister must deeply respect each person and not presume that what happened in the past will happen in the same way now. The best we can do is to quote some of the unsolicited responses that we have received.

There may be an immediate response or it may be considerably delayed. A sister went to the Eucharist many hours after being prayed with for a healing of memories filled with deep resentment.

> "The impact of all this didn't really hit me till about mid-Mass and then followed the tears of love, gratitude, repentance, humility for God's understanding love. Need I say, I can't ever doubt his great love for me. Father, please help me praise and thank him for this wonderful favor."

A young woman did not respond to inner healing prayer. She was cold, heavily burdened and unable to remember her early years which were the times when she was seriously wounded. But she wrote the next day:

"I want to share with you the joy and thanksgiving I have in the healing the Lord did when you prayed with me. At first, I didn't think very much was going to happen but that I felt good. But the Lord showed me how rebellious I am and how I was blinded by self-pity and martyrdom. But praise God now my eyes can see a little better. There was of course initial unveilings and release of anger I didn't know was the cause of my upsets. Anger, I regret to say, to God. But then, of course, came the true acceptance that all my life Jesus was there. I began to feel it more and more each day—till it just dawned on me, I could feel him in my memories and now I realize that his presence was there always—isn't it truly wonderful to know Jesus is always with us. I am so glad. It has really FREED me."

Some wrote of immediate experiences of being healed and freed:

"Since then, I have felt the tender touch of Jesus burning deep within my heart. He has opened me to receive him."

"I experienced the power of the Lord cutting through my insides and touching my heart."

One man who had prayed for a healing many times wrote that nothing had happened in earlier prayers. He now knows that God's love had penetrated his past and knew a truth that:

"It's not my huffing, puffing and pushing but openness to the Lord's work. I've learned I have to be gentle on myself to receive a healing. I also see a definite correlation between my being open to receive

a healing and the gentleness with which those ministering treat me."

A sister experienced a deep healing of her heart
which freed her from attitudes of inferiority and insecuri-
ty. In prayer she realized that from her earliest years she
had been gripped by the fear that she would be a mongo-
loid child because of her eyes and so she had competed
desperately in all areas of success to prove her self-worth.
When this basic fear finally surfaced, she asked to know
the Father's choice of her in all her childhood memories
and she proclaimed to us that she was experiencing the
deep love of God for her in just those memories.

There is always the possibility that so-called healings
can be just an emotional escape from the problems. Our
experience is that people become more realistic as a result
of healing prayers. One sister saw her life pattern as escaping from her community and realized in prayer that
her healing would only be completed in her own community. She responded:

"My life must be formed by my community as it is. I
receive my healing by working through the real community that exists. It is like the garden I tend. The
weeds are as real as the flowers; I have to tend the
whole garden: weeds and flowers."

Another woman wrote of being able to face real life
for the first time:

"But now like Lazarus I'm not bound anymore. I
truly feel I received an inner healing of my whole
being. My memory of my bitterness, discouragement
and depression. I remember the past now, but there is

no pain, but joy, real joy! I know he loves me and I love him. I can look at the sky now and see blue clouds, sun. Before my eyes tended to be glued to the ground because I was 'dirt.' I want to live not die, to go out not withdraw, to love my body not destroy it, to love not to hate. I know I'm still human and reality will hit me again, but God has changed me and my attitudes. I'm a free daughter of God. Father, help me praise God!"

Can we prove that all these healing experiences were valid and enduring? We can only say that we knew the people before and we observed them during the period of healing prayers and we know them now to be freer and more peaceful. They speak words such as the following:

"The proof I have that the Spirit really came as you prayed over me is the deep, deep, peace, joy, over-flowing gratitude and wholeness in my innermost being. There was a part of me that wasn't God's, an inner propensity toward self-satisfaction and self-gra-tification that is very difficult to explain. Many years of self-indulgence and lack of mortification made the conquest of this habitual selfishness seem like an im-possibility. But the Spirit has made me whole—whol-ly his so that now I am gratitude, joy, peace, love."

These graces certainly don't mean the end of prob-lems and difficulties but the problems can be handled with new freedom as one person wrote:

"I don't seem to have many problems now. I'm really sure God loves me and I love him so much. I can go to him with my problems, when I couldn't before and somehow I know he helps me. I'm really happy now —I haven't felt this way in such a long time.

"It's really a great feeling to know, *really know*, that God loves you. And what's even better is knowing how much you love him back. I seem to love God so much. I can't begin to tell anyone how much—and this time it's going to last."

Each person is different, each situation of follow-up or ongoing support is different. But, we have found our vitality is standing on the word of the Lord: "See I make all things new" (Rev. 21:5). He makes our hearts new, he gives us power for new life and new hope in all our relationships. If we are open to the healing power of Jesus as Lord of our lives there is not one relationship which cannot be renewed, not one person to write off as hopeless. All can be touched and made vibrant in love. But, this is an ongoing process never fully completed. Our prayer for one another should be that of Saint Paul: "May Christ dwell in your heart, may he be the root and foundation of your being." (Eph. 3:14-15)

# VI
# The Healing Community

The Gospel calls us to be formed into healing communities. It is in such communities that the healing described in the earlier chapters will flow in the fulness described. The Lord intends his Body to be joined together in love and his love to be manifested through the ongoing gift of healing. A true Eucharistic community would continually be in the process of being healed. It would stand in faith on the communion prayer proclaimed by the congregation at every Catholic Eucharistic liturgy: "O Lord, I am not worthy that you should enter under my roof; say but the word and I shall be healed." It would be one with the presiding priest's communion prayer: "Lord Jesus Christ, with faith in your love and mercy I eat your body and drink your blood. Let it not bring me condemnation but health in mind and body."

Our work has emphasized the minister's or ministers' role in inner healing. We now concentrate on the dimension of the community's role. The faith necessary to be healed is not confined to the faith of the person seeking healing and that of the minister. There can be a vital resource of faith in the community. This is well illustrated in one of the earliest healings presented to us by the synoptic authors, Matthew, Mark and Luke.

"Then he reentered the boat, made the crossing and

came back to his own town. There the people at once
brought to him a paralyzed man lying on a mat.
When Jesus saw *their* faith, he said to the paralytic,
"Have courage, son, your sins are forgiven" (Mt. 9:1-
2; Mk. 2:3-5; Lk. 5:17-20).

No doubt the evangelists writing as Christian be-
lievers tend to cover the use of faith in terms of the specifically Christian faith in Christ as a divine person. Nevertheless, all three writers emphasize faith beyond that of
the individual seeking healing to those at least attending
him but not so far as to include the scribes who are presented as hostile.

During these past four years, we have observed the
role of the community's faith in the inner healing of semin-
arians. In prayers for healing we are able to pray with a
group of men who will live with and support the one being
healed in the days to come. The faith of the individual is
interrelated with the faith of the community from the
initial calling forth of faith to the sustaining of it over long
periods of time. One seminarian remarked the importance
of being trusted by those who prayed with him at his point
of greatest weakness. He stated that "they believed in my
being healed more than I did and they relied on it by asking me to support them in ways I was never before capable
of doing." Another seminarian remarked that he could
experience the healing presence of the Lord in the group
praying before he first asked for prayer. He found himself
being transformed into a man of expectant faith as he
joined into the faith expression of others. Up until that
time, he believed the doctrine of Christianity and he relied
on God's providence somehow, at some time to care for
everything and work it all out. When he prayed with a

group gathered together in expectant faith, he came alive to a new dimension of faith and expected to be healed of his scrupulosity.

In discussion with those who ministered healing to others within the seminary community, there was a general consensus that the ministers let the light, which healed them and is healing them, flow forth to bring healing to others. The minister is first a vessel that overflows with the Lord's peace before he is an instrument of that healing.

To the extent that true Christian communities are being formed we can expect the growing presence of healing power. In his excellent work on Christian community, Max Delespesse defines community as:

> "An organic and stable fraternal association of persons accepting responsibility for one another through sharing both what they are and what they have in order to bring about the union of mankind."[27]

A true community is one where the giving of each member is to the point where each accepts responsibility for the other and shares his very self. The teaching of the New Testament is that there is special power available to those who come together in the name of Jesus. The Church is meant to have the note of togetherness, fellowship or "koinonia." This koinonia is essential to Church and those ministries that do not flow from togetherness in the Lord will necessarily lack power.

Reverend Graham Pulkingham has witnessed to this truth in his book on The Church of the Reedemer in Houston, Texas.[28] It was in the total gift of the leaders to each other under the Lordship of Jesus that the gifts of power were received.

The clearest passage on koinonia is found in Matthew 18:20: "Where two or three are gathered in my name, there am I in their midst." This reflects the belief of the Church in the power of common prayer, not necessarily of the whole Church; an assembly of two or three, as long as gathered in the name of the Lord, is sufficient. Thus, the Christian community believed in the Lord's teaching that he is especially present in power when they were gathered in his name. A close analysis of the Johannine passages of power reveals this koinonia element. Jesus addressing the apostles in the last discourse says: "whatever you ask in my name I will do so as to glorify the Father in the Son" (Jn. 16:23); "Anything you ask me in my name I will do" (Jn. 14:13-14). "If you live in me and my words stay part of you, you may ask what you will—it will be done for you" (Jn. 15:7); "I give you my assurance, whatever you ask the Father, he will give you in my name" (Jn. 16:23). These statements are addressed to the apostles as a body gathered together. These promises come after the years of molding the apostles into a unity whereby they could be the foundation of the Church. Saint Paul describes the ideal of Christian unity in his letter to the Ephesians: "make every effort to preserve the unity which has the Spirit as its origin and peace as its binding force" (Eph. 4:3).

The Epistles of John treats this fellowship (koinonia): "But if we walk in the light as he is in the light, we have fellowship with one another and the blood of his Son Jesus cleanses us from all sin" (1 Jn. 1:7). This fellowship is both the sign and the continuing source of the ongoing power of the redemptive work in Jesus.

Experience teaches us that insofar as people grow in the unity of the Spirit and in the oneness of the heart and mind of Jesus, they are endowed with power. This power includes the healing power to make whole and make one. But this only happens where leaders are truly given people. They prefer others to themselves. They have let go of hangups, secrecy and rationalization for failures. They are given people as the Lord was and his power becomes theirs.

In addition to the gift of healing from the Lord we are also talking about an environment for loving support. As presented earlier, there is a necessary level of affirmation which people need in order to let go of security devices, make decisions of commitment and step in faith. This supportive environment is also necessary for maintaining health and growing into the completion of healing. Max Delespesse describes this process as follows:

> "But love, the force of God in us, the dynamism through which we encounter God, begins with acceptance. All the people the Lord has us meet along the way need to be accepted by us as they are, and not as we would like them to be. They need to feel totally and fully accepted as they are. They need to be sure of never being judged. Everyone has a road to travel, but the plan that God devises for each one to achieve adult stature, is probably not the plan that we ourselves would like to make. Therefore, a love which is strong, healing and productive becomes a love which is infinitely respectful. We never know what we are bringing to fruition.

> "To really achieve mutual acceptance in our communities we must learn to know others and to let ourselves be known by them.

> "Without knowledge love is impossible. Moreover it is only by loving that we really know. The members

of a community choose, consequently, to reveal themselves in depth to others, so as to be known by them in truth and humility. They do not screen themselves behind a facade because they are convinced of the need they have for one another. This reciprocal knowledge, which is itself only possible with a great deal of love, enables them to love one another more, to give their lives for one another, to heal one another. Such is the strength of a community.[29]

This environment is well analyzed by Stephen Clark in his book *Building Christian Communities*. He defines a basic Christian community as: "an environment of Christians which can provide for the basic needs of its members to live the Christian life." [30] He explains the environment requirement as follows:

"There must be interaction between the people in the social grouping that is personal, that is, relationship-oriented and not just task-oriented."[31]

What Mr. Clark is pointing up is the need for primary relationships centered on Christ: relationships based on personal knowledge, regular sharing of lives and face to face encounters in which each is accepted as a person of value and where each is giving and receiving support.

We are learning many things about healing within community. The Spirit of Jesus alive in our hearts is a Spirit seeking unity. The Epistle to the Ephesians is the Epistle of Christian unity. The Spirit is there presented as continually moving all members toward what promotes peace and harmony. People hear these words and know they are true. Yet, they find it difficult to respond in faith, a faith expecting this force of unity to be efficacious. We have found that prayer which visualizes this power of the

Spirit can be very powerful in healing relationships among individuals and factions within a community.

When men and women are in touch with the Spirit of God in their lives, they know the restlessness of that Spirit to love and unite in love, to believe in both self and the other and to hope for newness of life and healing of relationships. We have seen such people break through to new unity when they are led in a prayer for healing of relationships.

We will summarize a typical prayer for a group. Frequently, the people are first told to visualize the Lord coming to them, touching them and embracing them. This visualization in prayer can be healing for to so visualize is to accept forgiveness and open to healing. Then the individuals are told to visualize the person with whom they are having the most difficult relationship. Once again, they visualize the Lord coming towards the person, reaching out, touching and embracing. As they visualize this, they know from within the Lord's forgiveness for the other. They recall the Lord's forgiveness for themselves and they open to forgiving the other and accepting forgiveness from him. Then they picture the Lord with arms around each of them slowly bringing them together. The Lord takes their arms and places them around each other and as they come together in an embrace of reconciliation he envelops them in a large embrace. If the persons involved have prayerfully and fully cooperated with this prayer they will know new healing which in subsequent actions can lead to full reconciliation.

This visualization process may seem to some to be too fictional and emotional. Actually, it is a true representation of the action of the Spirit and grace in our lives. It is emotional to the extent that emotional problems have caused the rupture. The degree of emotion in a solution to personal problems is directly related to the degree of emotion that was involved in the rupture. Emotionalism is a form of sentimentality in which the emotion involved exceeds in substantial disproportion what is justified by the facts of the situation. Tears and exclamations of joy are to be expected when there are breakthroughs unto healing. Joyful embracing by those who know new healing in their relationship is a sign of the Kingdom and a delight to behold.

In February 1974, we observed twelve hundred prayer group leaders gathered in Washington Township, New Jersey go deep within themselves in repentance, open to the healing love of the Lord, respond to the call of giving and receiving forgiveness, open to the Lord bringing the other within themselves and finally accept the reconciliation. The gymnasium was so silent that one participant said it was the first time she "had ever heard silence." The silence gradually gave way to softly spoken praise, then gentle song, then a release of joy and thanksgiving that continued for twenty minutes. Those present observed beautiful emotions being expressed; there wasn't any emotionalism to be seen. Something new and beautiful had happened; old relationships had new power and hope and those who were strangers to each other knew a mysterious sense of being brothers and sisters in Jesus Christ, The Lord.

# VII
# The Spirit to the Churches

What is the Spirit of God saying to us as we reflect on the meaning of inner healing? We hear the message as urging us to know a new fullness of love. We hear a word that does not destroy or demolish but which unites and completes. We hear a word of hope for a people torn and ravaged by the violence of the times.

The Spirit says to us that "there is one Lord, one faith, one baptism; one God and Father of all, who is over all, and works through all and is in all" (Ephesians 4:5-6). God is the God of medicine, psychiatry and counselling. The Fatherhood of God seeks in love to embrace and bring healing to all his hurting children. The Lord is the one Lord of all whose lordship is not just limited to today but which extends back into our histories, into our internal wounds, back to the beginning of our lives. The Father's tenderness and healing love is so beyond our own that we resist believing in such a deep, personal, healing love for ourselves.

But today, we must believe. For God's people have been ravaged by the violence of society. They have experienced rejection, alienation, psychological abuse, emotional warfare, and emptiness of life as never before. The new mass society with its frenzied activity, constant mobility and technological traumas of "Future Shock" is leaving behind a carnage of hollow men and women.

God cares! And the Spirit of God reaches to these children to comfort and heal them in a way that preserves the good in our scientific approaches but which completes them with new power. The call of the Spirit is to believe in this great love, to believe that God not only can but will heal with this love and to respond in expectant faith.

Faith is so crucial. The Spirit calls us to the Gospel dimension of faith. This is not just doctrinal faith which accepts propositions and formulations of beliefs as true. It is not just providential faith which believes in the overall providence of God that he sees that everything will work out in the end. It is expectant faith which expects God's saving love to operate in my life here and now. This is the faith which releases God's power. This is the faith that pulsates in the writings of the New Testament Church. The Spirit is not so concerned whether we believe that the wonders of the Apostolic Church are happening anew today as he is that we expect the saving Lord to be involved powerfully and lovingly in our lives. The Spirit is ever the same and yet ever new. We cannot understand this mystery, but we can understand that this means that what God is doing today is at once the same thing as he did before and a new work which we have never seen before. We are not to dwell on the work itself be it yesterday's or today's. We are to look to the Lord and expect him to be present.

The Spirit is the Spirit of Jesus who makes Jesus present in power in our midst. This Spirit calls us to expectant faith that reaches to Jesus as our healer. Our faith should not be preoccupied with wonders but with the Lord who is acting in our midst.

The Spirit speaks to the Churches. He calls them to a new fullness of life. He affirms the good of using the gifts of God to develop competent leaders and professional specialists in so many areas, to organize to better serve the poor, to research and study the meaning of the Scriptures and those traditions developed under the inspiration of the Spirit. But, this Spirit has this against the Churches: they so easily forsake their greatest source of power, the life-giving power that flows from the Lordship of Jesus. The center of the Churches' lives becomes the structure, the activities, the teaching or the professional leadership; good as these things are in perspective, they cannot give life to God's people.

The Spirit says wake up and believe. Get up and work while there is light. Be compassionate as I your God am compassionate; heal my people, my chosen people whom I love and desire to gather under my wing. Heal them!

# Appendix

We have attempted to emphasize the sacredness of every person so that the inner healing process does not violate that dignity at any point. The most likely time that a minister will violate a person is when he is unable to respond to the Gospel standards. The minister will be tempted to become demanding and even abrasive out of misguided zeal to see the person healed. Below are ten cautions designed to prevent such a misapplication of this book's teaching.

(1) Some people are too bound to be able to forgive or to receive forgiveness. They cannot even decide for the forgiveness because their negative feelings are too much in control. This must be respected. Frequently, they have to be given time or they need to be strengthened in other areas before deep healing prayer can take place.

(2) Many persons in need of deliverance or healing are reluctant to seek it. There can be a temptation to pressure them into asking for help. We should be cautious. God so respects man's free will that he leaves man free to say no. We should do likewise. The fullness of God's plan for any man cannot come about through force. It must be through free choice and commitment. The defenses people are using may be necessary for them at this stage. We should be cautious about too quickly challenging them.

(3) People don't know everything that is buried in their subconscious. They are embarrassed by emotions

that surface—frequently in areas they prided themselves as mature and advanced. We must respect them, acknowledging that what is buried in us alive remains alive until handled and a virtuous life built on this foundation usually cannot bring healing without some release of specific memories.

(4) People are also embarrassed and frustrated when they exhibit strong negative feelings and yet they don't know why. We should respect them and express our understanding. We can assure them that at the right time they will know the roots and causes. The Lord's time is a guiding concept. This situation is frequently present when religious people discover they are passionately angry at God.

(5) Some lack sufficient faith and feel guilty about it. We should never burden others because of this lack of faith. Faith is a gift. We are to pray regularly that our faith increase and we are to live as much as possible relying on the faith we do have. Therefore, when a person in need is lacking in faith, we do not demand he make a will power effort to believe. We affirm what he does have and thank God for it. We ask the Father for an increase in faith and we expect that it will be given. We ask the person what faith he has and then encourage and support him in living out that faith.

(6) People often feel inferior when seeking help. It is important that we create an environment of equality among all present. We should not have a "patient chair" with the "doctors" gathered around peering and ready to diagnose and prescribe. The environment should be marked by love for God and one another. The participants are grateful servants of the Lord.

(7) People come to us after or while also receiving professional help. Sometimes the professional care is very

good, sometimes it is ineffective but still important to the client, and on occasion it is harmful. We should strive to affirm the good in all the assistance people are receiving and wherever possible create an environment of cooperative assistance.

(8) When a person has experienced new life and new hope through the power of the Holy Spirit, his expectations tend to soar. He expects the fullness of healing today. Ordinarily this does not happen. Orderly progression over a period of time is usually God's way. The person may become discouraged. We should help him to recognize the good that has already happened in his life and praise God for it. Then we can help him to see that the God who began a good work will bring it to completion.

(9) People sometimes proclaim a healing and then begin to experience the same old hurts they thought were healed. The person must be respected and supported, assured that he is not a failure just because there is clearly a long process ahead.

(10) When people know new hope and life through meeting a saving Lord in their personal lives, they establish a close relationship with those who served as instruments. It is important that the ministers realize this and give themselves to ongoing care for such people. There usually are follow-up needs for encouragement, concern and presence. Sometimes, additional sessions of prayer and counselling are necessary. The ministers should endeavor to project how and by whom these needs can be met before they undertake deep healing prayer with any person. In practice, the minister will experience the Lord's love for his people and this love will continue to motivate the minister to care lovingly for the flock of the Good Shepherd.

# Notes

1. These cases were selected from among others because they most directly influenced us in understanding the working of God's healing power.

2. Mt. 4:23; Mt. 9:35; Mk. 6:56; Acts 10:30. *The New American Bible* used herein for all scripture quotations translates the first two references as "cured the people of every disease and sickness" and "cured every disease and sickness." The meaning of these four statements is not to maintain a scientific inclusion of every person or every known disease but to proclaim the large encompassing healing ministry of Jesus.

3. We should not use these texts as we would a medical record of healings. There are thirty-four apparently separate healings mentioned and approximately eighteen of these are mentioned by two or more evangelists.

4. Morton Kelsey, *Healing and Christianity*, Harper & Row, New York, 1973, pp. 345, 358-9.

5. The citations listed show a consistency of using the Greek for casting out whenever the devil or his equivalent is the object and using the Greek for healing whenever the people are the object. Therefore, the more determining factor is the designation of the spirits.

6. There is an impressive consistency in distinguishing the unclean (akathartos) spirits from the evil (peneros) spirits. Two classes are definitely reflected in the Greek and therefore support our thesis.

7. Kelsey, *Healing and Christianity*, p. 299.

8. See Luke 12:35-36: "Take care, then, that your light is not darkness. If your whole body is lighted up and not partly in darkness, it will be as fully illuminated as when a lamp shines brightly for you."

9. The individual healings are contained in the 3rd, 9th, 14th, 16th, 20th and 28th chapters. The collective healings are mentioned in the 2nd, 5th, 6th, 8th, 14th, 19th and 28th chapters of the Acts of the Apostles.

10. Paul Tournier, *A Place For You*, New York, Harper & Row, 1968.

11. Trina Paulus, *Hope For The Flowers*, Newman Press, Paramus, 1972.

12. See Keith Miller *The Becomers*, Word Books, Publisher, Waco, Texas, 1973 for an excellent application of these Freudian concepts within a Christian framework.

13. See Thomas A. Harris *I'M OK YOU'RE OK*, Harper & Row, New York, 1967. This book is very useful to anyone engaged in counselling or inner healing ministry.

14. Henri Nouwen, J.M., *The Wounded Healer, Ministry In Contemporary Society*, Doubleday & Co., Inc., Garden City, New York, 1972.

15. Kelsey, *Healing and Christianity*, p. 212.

16. See Milton Mayeroff, *On Caring*, Perennial Library, Harper & Row Publishers, New York, 1972 for an excellent presentation on affirming the good in others to produce personal growth.

17. The works of Carl Rogers are excellent sources for learning the importance of reflecting back within the scope of non-directive counselling. For the purposes of this book, the most useful resource is *On Becoming A Person*, A Therapist's view of Psychotherapy, Houghton Mifflin Co., Boston, 1961.

18. Merlin R. Carothers, *Prison to Praise*, Logos International, Plainfield, New Jersey, 1970. *Power in Praise*, Logos International, Plainfield, New Jersey, 1972.

19. *The Roman Ritual* translated and edited by Rev. Philip Weller, Bruce Publishing Co., Milwaukee, Wis., 1952.

20. The best current work on possession is: Rev. John J. Nicola *Diabolical Possession and Exorcism*, Tan Books and Publishers Inc., Rockfield, Ill., 1974. For a succinct statement on possession and its relationship to evil influence and disease see Karl Rahner, Herbert Vorgrimler, *Theological Dictionary*, Herder and Herder, New York, 1965, p. 365.

21. Two books are recommended for a better understanding of deliverance: Don Basham, *Deliver Us From Evil*, Chosen Books, Washington Depot, Connecticut, 1972 and Michael Harper, *Spiritual Warfare*, Hodder and Stoughtow, London, 1970.

22. *L'OSSERVATORE ROMANO*, "Deliver Us From Evil," November 23, 1972, pp. 3, 12.

23. *The Roman Ritual*, p. 641, specifies that a priest "expressly and particularly authorized by the Ordinary" for formal exorcism should "be of mature years and revered not alone for his office, but for his moral qualities."

24. Paul Tillich, *The New Being*, Charles Scribner's & Sons, New York, 1955, pp. 38-39.

25. Cf. 1 Corinthians 13: "Be on your guard, stand firm in the faith and act like men. In a word be strong."

26. Doctor Paul Tournier records the following experience of the power of faith in psychoanalysis:

"While I pray in silence, she tells of terrible emotional shocks suffered in childhood, which have weighed on her mind all her life. I cannot, of course, recount them here but what I want to point out is that they are the sort of repressed memories which psychoanalytical technique sometimes helps to bring out into the daylight but never as quickly as this.

When I thanked Florence for the trust she had shown in me by being so frank, she replied simply that what had made it possible was that she had come with me into the presence of God."

Paul Tournier, *The Healing of Persons*, Harper & Row, New York, 1965, pp. 236-237.

27. Max Delespesse, *The Church, Community Leaven and Life-Style*, The Catholic Center of Saint Paul University, Ottowa, 1969, p. 4.

28. Reverend Graham Pulkingham, *Gathered For Power*, Morehouse Bartow Co., New York, 1972.

29. Delespesse, *The Church, Community Leaven and Life-Style*, p. 26.

30. Stephen Clark, *Building Christian Communities*, Ave Maria Press, Notre Dame, Ind., 1972, p. 70.

31. Clark, *Building Christian Communities*, p. 70.